MW00882221

Law
and
Gospel

ROBERT M. HILLER
&
MICHAEL HORTON

Law and Gospel
Robert M. Hiller and Michael Horton

© 2023 Sola Media
13230 Evening Creek Drive
Suite 220–222
San Diego, CA 92128

All rights reserved. No part of this book may be
reproduced or transmitted in any form or by any means,
electronic or mechanical, including photocopying,
recording, or by any information storage and retrieval system,
without permission in writing from the publisher.

Design and Creative Direction by Metaleap Creative
Cover Design by Karly Steenholdt

Printed in the United States of America

First Printing—February 2023

CONTENTS

Introduction

HAVE YOU CONSIDERED how Scripture attributes all of God's works to his speech? Although the phrase *word of God* has various meanings in Scripture, it is "never simply a sound, but a power, no mere information but also an accomplishment of His will. By this word Jesus quiets the sea, Mk. 4:38, heals the sick, Mt. 8:16, casts out demons, 9:6, raised the dead, Luke 7:14, etc."[1] God's word "goes forth" like a powerful army. The voice of the Great King accomplishes unfailingly whatever he intends. Before time and the existence of angels or worlds, there was the unbegotten Father begetting without beginning the eternal Son as his consubstantial Word together with the Spirit. The Son is God's Word in the essence that he shares equally and undividedly with the Father. Consistent with this eternal procession, all of God's external works are accomplished by the Father, mediated through the Son. Every word is made effectual by the Spirit, who works within creation to bring about the performance of what has been "worded" to be. And all of God's powerful speech can be gathered under two types: command and promise; good works and good news; law and gospel.

In this booklet, White Horse Inn hosts Michael Horton and Bob Hiller explain this essential biblical distinction, which was recovered in the sixteenth-century Reformation. We associate the Reformation with the *solae* ("alones"): salvation in Christ alone, revealed in Scripture alone, received through faith alone by God's grace alone to his glory alone. Yet the distinction between law and gospel is as nuclear to the Reformers' emphasis—and, more importantly, to Scripture itself.

---

1 From chapter 10 (section 56) of Herman Bavinck's *Gereformeerde Dogmatiek*, 3rd unaltered ed., vol. 4 (Kampen: J. H. Kok, 1918), this excerpt was translated by Nelson D. Kloosterman as "Law-Gospel Distinction and Preaching," 2.

LAW AND GOSPEL

CHAPTER ONE
Defining Law & Gospel

Michael Horton

WHAT IS THE LAW?

God's law is not only a part of the Old Testament that prescribed detailed regulations and rites for enjoying long life in God's holy land. It is also *everything* in Scripture that commands. The law announces God's moral will. It reveals God's righteousness.

God's word of law also executes judgment. It creates a people bound to him. This is called a covenant. In a covenant of law, the servant swears an oath to obey based on conditional promises: "Do this and you will live." That is exactly what God said to Adam and Eve: "In the day that you eat of [the forbidden fruit], you shall surely die" (Gen. 3:5). To this, they led the chorus of birds and beasts in shouting, "Amen!" —swearing their covenant oath to all that God had said. Our first parents were not created neutral but in true righteousness and holiness. They could say from the heart, "Oh how I love your law! It is my meditation all the day" (Ps. 119:97). This word from God's lips matched perfectly their natural disposition.

Yet there was a trial to fulfill in order to merit the covenant reward that God promised: the right to be confirmed in blessedness by eating from the sacramental Tree of Life. God's liberality was on full display: "The LORD God took the man and put him in the garden of Eden to work it and keep it. And the LORD God commanded the man, saying, *'You may surely eat of every tree of the garden'*" (Gen. 2:15, emphasis added). God's lavish provision lacked nothing. In fact, there were more varieties of food than Adam and Eve could ever use. But God forbade them to eat from one tree, saying "of the tree of the knowledge of good and evil you shall not eat, for in the day that you eat of it you shall surely die'" (Gen. 2:15–17).

Mysteriously, Adam and Eve—God's image and likeness—turned away from God's word. They gave ear to the word of Satan and became traitors. Declaring independence from God and their ability to decide for themselves what was good, they fell under the curse of the law. Since Adam was the covenantal head of the human race, all of us are born guilty and corrupt (Ps. 51:5; Rom. 5).

God's law then constituted the nation of Israel as God's people. Having delivered them from Egypt, God assumed royal sovereignty over the nation and issued his decrees. The people swore allegiance to him at Mount Sinai. "All this we will do," they declared with one voice as Moses splashed them with blood: "And Moses took the blood and threw it on the people and said, 'Behold the blood of the covenant that the LORD has made with you in accordance with all these words'" (Exod. 24:8).

By delivering his offspring and giving them the promised land, God fulfilled his promise to Abraham. Joshua writes, "Not one word of all the good promises that the LORD had made to the house of Israel had failed; all came to pass" (Josh. 21:45). But now it was Israel's turn to swear an oath, renewing the promise their fathers had made at Sinai. Given the land by grace alone, Israel was now on trial like Adam in the garden. The people again swore, "All this we will do":

> But Joshua said to the people, "You are not able to serve the LORD, for he is a holy God. He is a jealous God; he will not forgive your transgressions or your sins. If you forsake the LORD and serve foreign gods, then he will turn and do you harm and consume you, after having done you good." And the people said to Joshua, "No, but we will serve the LORD." Then Joshua said to the people, "You are witnesses against yourselves that you

have chosen the LORD, to serve him." And they said, "We are witnesses." (Josh. 24:19–22).

Indeed, as the story unfolds, Israel imitates Adam: "Like Adam, Israel broke my covenant" (Hos. 6:7). The prophets were sent as God's lawyers, representing him in the courtroom as he put Israel on trial. On the basis of the people's covenant oath, "All this we will do," Israel was condemned. Yet *God* swore an oath that he would fulfill the greater promise to Abraham, which goes all the way back to Genesis 3:15: He will save his people by grace and bring them into a far greater land in the everlasting Sabbath. It is always the word of law that brings the story to a standstill; but God's word of gospel—the "new thing" he will do—always keeps it moving again.

Everything in Scripture, in both the Old and New Testaments, that commands us to do something is "law." It is good, reflecting God's righteous will that brings blessing and joy. But commands cannot create the reality of which they speak. God's law can only "tell it like it is," arraigning transgressors before God's throne. In a conditional covenant, the law only condemns the wicked.

In the covenant of grace, however, Christ is the mediator, and the promises are not merely of long life on a piece of land in the Middle East but of life with God in his everlasting rest. God's moral law is still normative for believers, but it cannot condemn us since its demands have been met fully by our representative head, Jesus Christ, who has born our sentence on the cross. Not the obedience of the people but the obedience of the faithful Son is the basis of this gracious covenant. It is God who swears the oath and the people receive the gift through faith. Instead of Moses splashing blood on the people in accordance with their oath, "All this we will do," Jesus sheds his own blood *for* the people in accordance with his oath, "All this I will do": "And he took bread, and when he had given thanks, he broke it and gave it to them, saying, 'This is my body, which is given for you. Do this in remembrance of me.' And likewise the cup after they had eaten, saying, 'This cup that is poured out for you is the new covenant in my blood'" (Luke 22:19–20).

The gospel is the second word that God speaks throughout Scripture.

WHAT IS THE GOSPEL?

In the opening salutation of Paul's letter to the Romans, the apostle summarizes the gospel he will unpack for them:

> The gospel of God, which he promised beforehand through his prophets in the holy Scriptures, concerning his Son, who was descended from David according to the flesh and was declared to be the Son of God in power according to the Spirit of holiness by his resurrection from the dead, Jesus Christ our Lord, through whom we have received grace and apostleship to bring about the obedience of faith for the sake of his name among all the nations, including you who are called to belong to Jesus Christ. (Rom. 1:1–6)

First, it is "the gospel of *God*." Theology is the study of God. God exists. He's independent, free, eternal, wholly satisfied in the joy of the Father, the Son, and the Spirit. Nothing is necessary to complete this communion, yet God decided to create others who are not God. What ensues is the history of the world, and it is about God. History's main object is the gospel of God: the announcement of God's purposes, promises, and achievements—not ours. The gospel is either irrelevant or offensive when we presuppose that we are at the center of the universe. Religion, morality, and spirituality are "from the people, by the people, and for the people." For those of us raised in this human-centered perspective, biblical faith can only seem foreign. Earlier generations of Christians confessed at least the substance of the first answer of the Westminster Shorter Catechism: "The chief end of man is to glorify God and to enjoy him forever."

However, today it seems like our chief end is knowing, glorifying, and enjoying ourselves. If religion or spirituality or a "personal relationship with Jesus" can help us with that goal, so much the better.

Ironically, our ultimate pleasure and satisfaction can only arrive as we turn away from ourselves and find God as the sun around which all reality orbits. We cannot live somewhere in between a God-centered and human-centered interpretation of reality. If God exists and he created everything (including us), then obviously we are not the center. God is the center. Struggling feverishly to find happiness, a young man in northern Africa tried just about everything, from self-indulgence to extreme asceticism. Only after reading Romans could this famous church father, Augustine, confess, "You have made us for yourself, O Lord, and our heart is restless until it rests in you."

Second, saying that God is the object of theology entails a strong claim: namely, that God can be *known*. Yet that is precisely Paul's claim here: "the gospel of God, *which he promised beforehand through his prophets in the holy Scriptures.*" God can be known because he has revealed himself. It doesn't matter what we find interesting, helpful, edifying, or inspiring. The god who is a projection of our experience, morality, and life projects is hardly worth our worship. There is no reason even to bother with the "God" question unless God is the center of the cosmos and has taken the initiative to reveal himself to us. If God doesn't reveal himself, we're just talking to ourselves in a god-like voice, spiritual ventriloquists who make our wooden partner speak the lines we have written for it.

Third, the main message of Scripture is "the gospel of God . . . *concerning his Son.*" Just as the Father spoke the world into being in, through and for the Son, his saving word is also about his Son. There is more in the Bible than the gospel. God reveals himself as Creator, Sustainer and Judge as well as the Savior and Shepherd of his people. God's moral will, as well as his saving will, is clearly exhibited. Yet, as Paul will argue, all people know by nature that God exists, and they know that they are obligated to this almighty and righteous God, so "they are without excuse" (1:20). What we need—what all of us need—is another word, something other than the general revelation of God's existence, power, glory, justice, and law. We need a saving revelation if we are to be reconciled to this Creator. For those who stand in a broken covenantal relationship with him, the only safe encounter with God is as he has revealed himself in Christ through the gospel.

Fourth, this gospel—the heart and soul of special revelation—is not about something that happens in our hearts. It is not an inner experience or subjective moral impulse but rather a revelation of historical events. This gospel of God concerns God's Son "who was *descended from David* according to the flesh and was declared to be the Son of God in power according to the Spirit of holiness by his *resurrection from the dead.*"

Fifth, although the gospel itself is an announcement about God's mighty deeds in Christ, apart from us, in history, the Spirit applies the benefits to us here and now through preaching and sacrament. Even those who were formerly not part of Israel, strangers to the covenants and promises, are now included as co-heirs with Christ. Effectually calling us through this gospel, the Spirit unites us to Christ for justification, sanctification, and future glorification. Paul concludes, "Jesus Christ our Lord, through whom we have received grace and apostleship to bring about the obedience of faith for the sake of his name among all the nations, *including you who are called to belong to Jesus Christ.*"

CHAPTER TWO

God's Two Words

Michael Horton

IT IS NOT A PASSAGE HERE OR THERE that gives us a distinction between the law and the gospel. Throughout Scripture we find it wherever wrath is contrasted with mercy—wherever being an enemy is contrasted with being reconciled, being a debtor with being an heir, being an employee with being a son, being dead and condemned with being alive and justified.

Today God still speaks his two words of law and gospel, judgment and justification. Romans unfolds in precisely this order. After the brief statement of his thesis, which outlines the gospel, Paul launches into his argument. Everyone, both Jew and Gentile, stands condemned by God's law (Rom. 1:18–3:20): "For by works of the law no human being will be justified in his sight, since through the law comes knowledge of sin" (3:20). In the very next verse, though, he shifts our attention to the gospel. He writes, "But now the righteousness of God has been manifested *apart from the law,* although the Law and the Prophets bear witness to it—the righteousness of God *through faith in Jesus Christ* for all who believe." Notice the distinction he draws between the law as the condemning verdict and "the Law and the Prophets." Consequently, the difference between law and gospel is not a difference between the Old and New Testaments. God's righteous demands and judgments are revealed clearly by Jesus and the apostles; the gospel thread, meanwhile, runs from Genesis 3:15 to the end of Malachi.

As Jews and gentiles share in condemnation, they also share in justification: "For there is no distinction: for all have sinned and fall short of the glory of

God, and are justified by his grace as a gift" (Rom. 3:22b–24). How can God do this? After all, Paul himself began, "For the wrath of God is revealed from heaven against all ungodliness and unrighteousness of men, who by their unrighteousness suppress the truth" (Rom. 1:18). And God's wrath isn't just for a few hedonists. Paul writes, "None is righteous, no, not one; no one understands; no one seeks for God. All have turned aside; together they have become worthless; no one does good, not even one" (Rom. 3:10–12).

We may wonder how God can condemn those who have never heard the gospel, but Scripture nowhere teaches that God judges people for rejecting the gospel. In fact, Paul has explained that everyone "stands condemned" because they have rejected even the knowledge of God made plain to them by nature. In this fallen condition "in Adam" (Rom. 5), all people are born into the world guilty and corrupt. We all "suppress the truth in unrighteousness"—whatever the content of God's self-revelation. For Paul's Jewish audience, the question was different. It was not "How can gentiles be held responsible for rejecting a gospel they never heard?" but "How can God justify the wicked?"—i.e. gentiles, etc. After all, "the LORD will by no means clear the guilty" (Nah. 1:3).

So how can Paul now say that God clears the guilty? If Paul had just said that this exoneration was a gift received by faith apart from the law, then the righteousness and justice of God would indeed seem to be threatened. But he adds, "through the redemption that is in Christ Jesus, whom God put forward as a propitiation by his blood, to be received by faith" (Rom. 24–25). It is not that God lowers the bar, accepting faith in the place of righteousness. Our faith is not the basis of salvation any more than our works. If it were, then the Son would never have had to become incarnate. Instead, the perfect discharge of our debt to justice is carried out by Christ, who fulfilled the law and bore its curses in our place: "It was to show his righteousness at the present time, so that he might be *just and the justifier* of the one who has faith in Jesus" (Rom. 3: 26, emphasis added). In Romans 5, Paul explains further that whereas all human beings share Adam's guilt and corruption, Christ is the new head in whom the law is perfectly fulfilled and the curse fully borne. The guilty are acquitted only because they are *not guilty* anymore before God.

My purpose is not to outline Romans but merely to show Paul's characteristic movement back and forth between the law and the gospel as God's two words. Again, these are external words, which means that it does not matter how you and I have judged ourselves or allowed others to judge us. Everyone is looking for "validation" today. A generation raised on social media is especially prone to believe what other people say about them, even those they have never met. But we are all full of nonsense, talking nonsense to ourselves and each other: false law and gospel. All that matters objectively is whether we are in Christ or still in Adam.

The law and the gospel conspire to extinguish every glimmer of spiritual and moral pride, as Paul concludes this part of his argument: "Then what becomes of our boasting? It is excluded. By what kind of law? By a law of works? No, but by the law of faith. For we hold that one is justified by faith apart from works of the law. . . . Do we then overthrow the law by this faith? By no means! On the contrary, we uphold the law" (Rom. 3:27–28, 31).

Romans 4–7 demonstrate that "we uphold the law" in two ways. First, the law is upheld because Christ fulfilled it and bore its judgment in our place. Second, because the law's good and righteous demands have been met, we are no longer under its condemnation. As far as the "old Adam" is concerned, the law is our hangman. But baptized into Christ, we are justified and the "new man" has been created in us (Rom. 6). The tension between our old and new identities continues throughout life, as Paul describes frankly, and autobiographically, in Romans 7. Yet even while he laments his failures, the apostle says, "I delight in the law of God in my inner being" (Rom. 7:21). This quotation of Psalm 119:97 does not describe us in the unregenerate condition that Paul describes in Romans 1–3. But this full concord of the law with the decree of justification has reconciled us to God's good words. That is precisely why we are so conflicted within ourselves: the objective work of God in us (justification and renewal) seems to be contradicted by how we feel and act. God redescribes us and in doing so creates the reality of which he speaks. To the one who receives Christ, the Father says, "I declare you righteous in my Son and because of this I am making you holy in my Son." But my little voice within disagrees—and so would people who know me well. Whose description should I believe? God's, of course, which he speaks in the gospel. Paul writes, "There is therefore now no condemnation for those who are in Christ Jesus" (Rom. 8:1). Because the law is fulfilled by Christ and imputed to us, it is not set aside but upheld.

Luther's Large Catechism follows the warp and woof of this argument in Romans closely:

> From this you perceive that the Creed is a doctrine quite different from the Ten Commandments; for the latter teaches indeed what we ought to do, but the former tells what God does for us and gives to us. Moreover, apart from this, the Ten Commandments are written in the hearts of all men; the Creed, however, no human wisdom can comprehend, but it must be taught by the Holy Ghost alone. 68 The latter doctrine [of the Law], therefore, makes no Christian, for the wrath and displeasure of God abide upon us still, because we cannot keep what God demands of us; but this [namely, the doctrine of faith] brings pure grace, and makes us godly and acceptable to God. 69 For by this knowledge we obtain love and delight in all the commandments of God, because here we see that God gives Himself entire to us, with all that He has and is able to do, to aid and direct us in keeping the Ten Commandments-the Father, all creatures; the Son, His entire work; and the Holy Ghost, all His gifts. (Art. III.66)

The Heidelberg Catechism summarizes the relationship of the law and the gospel in a similar way:

Q. 60: "How are you righteous before God?

Only by true faith in Jesus Christ. Although my conscience accuses me that I have grievously sinned against all God's commandments, have never kept any of them, and am still inclined to all evil, yet God, without any merit of my own, out of mere grace, *imputes* to me the perfect satisfaction, righteousness, and holiness of Christ. He grants these to me *as if I had never had nor committed any sin, and as if I myself had accomplished all the obedience which Christ has rendered for me,* if only I accept this gift with a believing heart.

Faith is not the ground of our receiving this gift of righteousness, since our faith could hardly fulfill the obedience God requires. But our faith is the sole way of receiving the gift:

Q. 61: Why do you say that you are righteous only by faith?

Not that I am acceptable to God on account of the worthiness of my faith, for only the satisfaction, righteousness, and holiness of Christ is my righteousness before God. I can receive this righteousness and make it my own by faith only.

Q. 62: But why can our good works not be our righteousness before God, or at least a part of it?

Because the righteousness which can stand before God's judgment must be absolutely perfect and in complete agreement with the law of God, whereas even our best works in this life are all imperfect and defiled with sin.

Q. 63: But do our good works earn nothing, even though God promises to reward them in this life and the next?

This reward is not earned; it is a gift of grace.

Q. 64: Does this teaching not make people careless and wicked?

No. It is impossible that those grafted into Christ by true faith should not bring forth fruits of thankfulness.

It is not only in Romans, then, that we see this contrast between what God does through his law and what he does through his gospel.

We face the danger, though, of embracing the gospel for our justification and then turning back to the law as the source and measure of our sanctification. Even when we heartily accept that we are saved by all that Christ has done, it is easy to assume that now our identity and growth in grace are the result of our oath, "All this we will do." But the law can do no more in our sanctification than it does in our justification, as John Murray explained: "No subject is more intimately bound up with the nature of the gospel than that of law and grace." He wrote, "In the degree to which error is entertained at this point, in the same degree is our conception of the gospel perverted." It is not the office of the law to save but to reveal God's righteous demands. Murray adds, "It must be appreciated that when Paul says in Romans 6:14, 'Ye are not under law but under grace,' there is the sharpest possible antithesis between 'under law' and 'under grace,' and that in terms of Paul's intent in this passage these are mutually exclusive. To be 'under law' is to be under the dominion of sin; to be 'under grace' is to be liberated from that dominion."[1]

Once we recognize the distinction, it becomes a filter for hearing God's speech throughout Scripture. Whatever God commands is right and true and good,

---

1   John Murray, *Principles of Conduct: Aspects of Biblical Ethics* (Grand Rapids: Eerdmans, 1957), 186.

but we are not. If the "new self" seeks *direction,* it is using the law lawfully. But if our conscience seeks *security* from the righteous wrath to come, it must be solely in the righteousness of Christ, received by faith.

Specifically, the *gospel* is that part of God's word that gives life. While everything that God says is true and impacts us, not everything that God says is *saving.* Sometimes God's speech brings judgment, disaster, fear, warning, and dread, Calvin reminds us.[2] He writes, "For although faith believes every word of God, it rests solely on the word of grace or mercy, the promise of God's fatherly goodwill," which is only realized in and through Christ.[3] "For in God faith seeks life," says Calvin, "which is not to be found in commandments or the pronouncement of penalties, but in the promise of mercy—and only a free promise."[4] The only safe route, therefore, is to receive the Father through the incarnate Son. Christ is the saving content of Scripture, the substance of its canonical unity.[5] In the same terms as Luther, Calvin teaches, "This is the true knowledge of Christ: if we take him as he is offered by the Father, namely, clothed with his gospel. For as he himself has been designated the goal of our faith, so we shall not run straight to him unless the gospel leads the way."[6]

Sometimes we think of the gospel merely as information or an offer, and one is saved by accepting it. This slides easily into the error that faith is our small contribution to our own salvation—and encourages emotional manipulation and marketing to "make a sale." But Paul says that the gospel, not our decision, is "the power of God unto salvation" (Rom. 1:16). We're familiar with the way news affects us. "You have cancer" isn't just medical information that you can take or leave; the news provokes its response. Similarly, when a doctor says with

2   John Calvin, *Institutes of the Christian Religion*, trans. Ford Lewis Battles, ed. John T. McNeill, 2 vols.. The Library of Christian Classics (Philadelphia: The Westminster Press, 1960), 3.2.7; 3.2.29. All references to the 1559 *Institutes* in this volume are from this edition.

3   Ibid., 3.2.28–30.

4   John Calvin, *Institutes* 3.2.29.

5   Ibid., 1.13.7.

6   Ibid., 3.2.6.

credible evidence, "Your cancer is gone," you want to shout it from the rooftop. Watering down the bad news is even more dangerous when our everlasting prognosis is at stake. There have always been false prophets who do this, like Judah's: "They have healed the wound of my people lightly, saying, 'Peace, peace,' when there is no peace" (Jer. 6:14).

A false diagnosis inevitably directs us to false cures. If we are good people who could be better, we need good advice and not good news. We need a better example to follow and not the incarnate God. We need a spiritual program and not a crucifixion and resurrection planted in the middle of history. If we are not enemies of God, we cannot be recipients of this news: "If *while we were enemies* we were reconciled to God by the death of his Son, much more, now that we are reconciled, shall we be saved by his life" (Rom. 5:10). If we're not "dead in trespasses and sins" (Eph. 2:1), then what does it mean that "even *when we were dead* in our trespasses, [God] made us alive together with Christ—by grace you have been saved" (Eph. 2:5)? The news itself generates dread or delight.

Of far greater impact than the testimony of mortals is the news coming from the Father concerning his Son, which the Holy Spirit makes effectual in our hearts. Just as God created the world out of nothing, without any assistance, he made Sarah's barren womb fruitful and gave Abraham the faith to believe the promise, "as it is written, 'I have made you the father of many nations'— in the presence of the God in whom he believed, who gives life to the dead and calls into existence the things that do not exist" (Rom. 4:16–17). This proclamation of the gospel that the Spirit creates faith out of nothing but unbelief and rebellion: "For God, who said, 'Let light shine out of darkness,' has shone in our hearts to give the light of the knowledge of the glory of God in the face of Jesus Christ" (2 Cor. 4:6). We do not find God by turning within or by climbing a ladder of speculation, mystical experience, or merit:

> But the righteousness based on faith says, "Do not say in your heart, 'Who will ascend into heaven?'" (that is, to bring Christ down) or 'Who will

descend into the abyss?'" (that is, to bring Christ up from the dead). But what does it say? "The word is near you, in your mouth and in your heart" (that is, the word of faith that we proclaim); because, if you confess with your mouth that Jesus is Lord and believe in your heart that God raised him from the dead, you will be saved (Rom. 10:6–9).

Far from suppressing our own speech, as I said above, God's word provokes and forms it. The proper response to God's law is, "All this we will do." The proper response to God's gospel is, "All this was done for me." Paul writes, "For with the heart one believes and is justified, and with the mouth one confesses and is saved" (Rom. 10:10). This is why common exhortations to "live the gospel" or even to "be the gospel" are foreign to the Bible. The gospel is precisely the opposite of what you or I can do or be. At the same time, those who say that Christianity is not about rules but about love fail to recognize that the law, as Jesus said, is a summary of what it means to love God and one's neighbor (Matt. 22:37–39). Whatever we hear that tells us to do something is law. Whenever we are told what God has done to save us in Christ, it is gospel. By definition, then, the gospel is not something you can *do* but an announcement of what has been *done for you by someone else.*

Yet faith is not only our response to God's gracious pledge but the fruit of it. The Heidelberg Catechism puts it succinctly:

> Q. 65: Since then we are made partakers of Christ and all his benefits by faith alone, where does this faith come from?
>
> The Holy Spirit creates it in our hearts by the preaching of the holy gospel and confirms it by the use of the holy sacraments.

This is why there must be preachers. Self-saviors need life coaches, motivators, cheerleaders, and sages. The gospel needs *heralds:* people who are called and sent by Christ through the church to bring the announcement to the ends of the earth. The gospel is not something that we can find; it finds us. Heralds are sent:

> How then will they call on him in whom they have not believed? And how are they to believe in him of whom they have never heard? And how are they to hear without someone preaching? And how are they to preach unless they are sent? As it is written, "How beautiful are the feet of those who preach the good news!" But they have not all obeyed the gospel. For Isaiah says, "Lord, who has believed what he has heard from us?" *So faith comes from hearing, and hearing through the word of Christ* (Rom 10:14–17, emphasis added).

Peter tells us, "[Y]ou have been born again, not of perishable seed but of imperishable, through the living and abiding word of God; for 'All flesh is like grass and all its glory like the flower of grass. The grass withers, and the flower fails, but the word of the Lord remains forever.' And this word is the good news that was preached to you" (1 Pet. 1:23–25). Consequently, wherever this word of law and gospel is preached, God himself judges and justifies, kills and makes alive, convicts and comforts. Throughout the book of Acts, the growth of the church is signaled by the report that "the word of God spread" (Acts 2:47; 6:7; 12:24; 19:20).

Just two days ago (as I write this), I picked up a book on self-improvement by a popular Hindu swami at the airport in Bangalore, India. The chapter titles were surprisingly similar to those of best-selling preachers in the U. S.: how to find inner peace, better relationships, and so forth. Much of what I read was good advice. But there was no gospel, of course, and that is often the case in popular Christianity today. Jesus often becomes no more than a moral example or life coach, helping us to have our best life now.

That kind of message may seem more cheerful than hellfire and brimstone preaching, but both are "law": telling us what we need to do to improve ourselves instead of telling us what God has done for us in Jesus Christ. Exhortations are still needed, but they do not give what they command. As J. Gresham Machen wrote,

> What good does it do to me to tell me that the type of religion presented in the Bible is a very fine type of religion and that the thing for me to do is just to start practicing that type of religion now? . . . I will tell you, my friend. It does me not one tiniest little bit of good. . . . What I need first of all is not exhortation, but a gospel, not directions for saving myself but knowledge of how God has saved me. Have you any good news? That is the question that I ask of you. I know your exhortations will not help me. But if anything has been done to save me, will you not tell me the facts?[7]

---

7   J. Gresham Machen, *Christian Faith in the Modern World* (New York: Macmillan, 1936), 57.

CHAPTER THREE

Law & Gospel as Reformation Distinctives

Michael Horton

THIS DISTINCTION BETWEEN LAW AND GOSPEL characterizes the churches of the Reformation. Luther explains "that the entire Scripture of God is divided into two parts: commands and promises."[1] We're always confusing them, he said, so anyone who can divide them properly should be given a doctorate! Luther's close associate Philip Melanchthon wrote, "All of Scripture is either Law or Gospel."[2] Calvin says that his critics "still do not observe that in the contrast between the righteousness of the law and of the gospel, which Paul elsewhere introduces, all works are excluded, whatever title may grace them [Gal. 3:11–12]. . . . [N]ot even spiritual works come into account when the power of justifying is ascribed to faith." It is the chief mistake of the medieval theologians, "who mingle their concoctions," to "interpret the grace of God not as the imputation of free righteousness but as the Spirit helping in the pursuit of holiness."[3] "And this shows how deluded the Sophists are," he writes, "who thought they had neatly got around all these absurdities [of confusing law and promise] by saying that works of their own intrinsic goodness are of no avail for meriting salvation but by reason of the covenant,

---

1   Luther, *Freedom of a Christian* translated by Timothy J. Wengert in *The Annotated Luther, Vol. I: The Roots of Reform* (Minneapolis: Fortress Press, 2015), 494.

2   Melanchthon, *Common Places: Loci Communes* (1521) (St. Louis: Concordia Publishing House, 2014), 94.

3   Calvin, *Institutes of the Christian Religion,* ed. John T. McNeill; tr. Ford Lewis Battles (Philadelphia: The Westminster Press, 1960), 3.11.14–15.

because the Lord of his own liberality esteemed them so highly."[4] This would of course vitiate Paul's argument that justification is based on Christ's complete fulfillment of the law and bearing of the curse. Instead, God just requires the slightest effort—"doing what lies within you"—to curry his mercy.

Wilhelm Niesel observes, "Reformed theology recognises the contrast between Law and Gospel, in a way similar to Lutheranism. We read in the Second Helvetic Confession: 'The Gospel is indeed opposed to the Law. For the Law works wrath and pronounces a curse, whereas the Gospel preaches grace and blessing.'"[5] On the first page of his *Commentary on the Heidelberg Catechism,* Zacharius Ursinus (the primary author of the catechism) states, "The doctrine of the church is the entire and uncorrupted doctrine of the law and gospel concerning the true God, together with his will, works, and worship."[6] He then elucidates what would become a typical Reformed statement of this law-gospel distinction, which was held in common with the Lutheran confession:

> The doctrine of the church consists of two parts: the Law, and the Gospel; in which we have comprehended the sum and substance of the sacred Scriptures. . . . Therefore, the law and gospel are the chief and general divisions of holy Scriptures, and comprise the entire doctrine comprehended therein . . . for the law is our schoolmaster, to bring us to Christ, constraining us to fly to him, and showing us what that righteousness is, which he has wrought out, and now offers unto us. But the gospel, professedly, treats of the person, office, and benefits of Christ. Therefore we have, in the law and gospel, the whole of the Scriptures comprehending the doctrine revealed from heaven for our salvation. . . . The law prescribes and enjoins what is to be done, and forbids what ought to be avoided: whilst the gospel announces the free remission of sin,

---

4 John Calvin, *Institutes,* op.cit., 3.17.3.

5 Wilhelm Niesel, *Reformed Symbolics: A Comparison of Catholicism, Orthodoxy and Protestantism,* tr. David Lewis (Edinburgh: Oliver and Boyd, 1962), 217.

6 Zacharius Ursinus, *Commentary on the Heidelberg Catechism* (P&R Publishing, from the 1852 Second American Edition), 1.

through and for the sake of Christ. . . . The law is known from nature; the gospel is divinely revealed. . . . The law promises life upon the condition of perfect obedience; the gospel, on the condition of faith in Christ and the commencement of new obedience.[7]

Ursinus's view had already been amplified by both Bullinger and Calvin, two Reformers who were widely known to disagree from time to time.[8] Theodore Beza made precisely the same point in his Confession, employing nearly the same terms and order of discussion as Ursinus, only adding the warning that "ignorance of this distinction between Law and Gospel is one of the principal sources of the abuses which corrupted and still corrupt Christianity."[9] In fact, the law-gospel distinction found its home in the covenant theology of the Reformed tradition. While differing on other aspects of this covenant theology, Calvinistic Baptists like Charles Spurgeon emphasized the same distinction:

> The man who can fully understand the word covenant is a theologian. That is the key of all theology—the covenant of works by which we fell, and the covenant of grace by which we stand, Christ fulfilling the covenant for us as our surety and representative, fulfilling it by the shedding of his blood, so leaving for us a covenant wholly fulfilled on our side, which is Christ's side, and only to be fulfilled now by God.[10]

The continental Reformed theologians during and immediately following the Reformation period were unanimous in this respect, and the significant structural place that they give to "Law and Gospel" in their systems is evident even as recently as Louis Berkhof's opening to his section "The Word of God

---

7   Ibid., 2–3.

8   See Michael S. Horton, "Calvin and the Law-Gospel Hermeneutic," *Pro Ecclesia,* (6:1, Winter, 1997), 27–42.

9   Theodore Beza, tr. James Clark, *The Christian Faith,* by Theodore Beza (Focus Christian Ministries Trust, 1992), 41ff.

10 Charles Spurgeon, "Feeding on the Bread of Life," New Park Street Pulpit, No. 2706, 601, at https://www.spurgeongems.org/sermon/chs2706.pdf.

as a Means of Grace."[11] J. Van Bruggen adds, "The Catechism, thus, mentions the gospel and deliberately does not speak of 'the Word of God,' because the Law does not work faith. The Law (Law and gospel are the two parts of the Word which may be distinguished) judges; it does not call a person to God and does not work trust in him. The gospel does that."[12]

William Perkins, the father of Elizabethan Puritanism, taught practical theology to generations of students through his *Art of Prophesying* (1592; 1606). In that work he asserts, "The basic principle in application is to know whether the passage is a statement of the law or of the gospel. For when the Word is preached, the law and the gospel operate differently. The law exposes the disease of sin, and as a side-effect stimulates and stirs it up. But it provides no remedy for it. . . . The law is, therefore, first in the order of teaching; then comes the gospel."[13] Even believers need to hear the Bible preached and applied with a clear view of this distinction. "Our sanctification is partial as yet. In order that the remnants of sin may be destroyed we must always begin with meditation on the law, and with a sense of our sin, in order to be brought to rest in the gospel."[14] All later declensions in English Puritanism and in Scotland, especially with the Marrow Controversy, resulted from confusion of the law and the gospel. Charles Bridges, an evangelical Anglican minister in the early eighteenth century noted especially for his work, *The Christian Ministry,* wrote:

The mark of a minister "approved unto God, a workman that needeth not

---

11 Berkhof, *Systematic Theology* (Grand Rapids: Eerdmans, 1979), 112: *The Law and the Gospel in the Word of God.* The Churches of the Reformation from the very beginning distinguished between the law and the gospel as the two parts of the Word of God as a means of grace. This distinction was not understood to be identical with that between the Old and the New Testament, but was regarded as a distinction that applies to both Testaments. There is law and gospel in the Old Testament and there is law and gospel in the New. The law comprises everything in Scripture which is a revelation of God's will in the form of command or prohibition, while the gospel embraces everything, whether it be in the Old Testament or the New, that pertains to the work of reconciliation and that proclaims the seeking and redeeming love of God in Jesus Christ. And each one of these two parts has its own proper function in the economy of grace.

12 J. Van Brugen, *Annotations on the Heidelberg Catechism,* (Neerlandia, Alberta: Inheritance Publications, 1998), 170.

13 William Perkins, *The Art of Prophesying* (Edinburgh: Banner of Truth, 1996), 54.

14 Ibid., 60.

to be ashamed," is, that he "rightly divides the word of truth." . . . This revelation is divided into two parts—the Law and the Gospel—essentially distinct from each other; though so intimately connected, that an accurate knowledge of neither can be obtained without the other.[15]

Spurgeon offers a succinct conclusion:

There is no point upon which men make greater mistakes than upon the relation which exists between the law and the gospel. Some men put the law instead of the gospel: others put the gospel instead of the law; some modify the law and the gospel, and preach neither law nor gospel: and others entirely abrogate the law, by bringing in the gospel. Many there are who think that the law is the gospel, and who teach that men by good works of benevolence, honesty, righteousness, and sobriety, may be saved. Such men do err. On the other hand, many teach that the gospel is a law; that it has certain commands in it, by obedience to which, men are meritoriously saved; such men err from the truth, and understand it not. A certain class maintain that the law and the gospel are mixed, and that partly by observance of the law, and partly by God's grace, men are saved. These men understand not the truth, and are false teachers. This morning I shall attempt—God helping me to show you what is the design of the law, and then what is the end of the gospel. The coming of the law is explained in regard to its objects: 'Moreover the law entered, that the offence might abound.' Then comes the mission of the gospel: 'But where sin abounded, grace did much more abound.'[16]

---

15 Charles Bridges, *The Christian Ministry* (Edinburgh: Banner of Truth, 1976), 222.

16 Charles Spurgeon, "Law and Grace" in the *New Park Street Pulpit,* No. 37, 285–86 at https://archive.org/details/SpurgeonNewParkPt01/page/n1/mode/2up.

LAW AND GOSPEL

CHAPTER FOUR

Confusing Law and Gospel

Robert M. Hiller

RECENTLY, MY FAMILY AND I ENJOYED A DELIGHTFUL evening out at our favorite Chinese restaurant. Full and happy, we received the bill with the expected prepackaged fortune cookies. I put no stock in such things, but we enjoy the cookies and the vague, optimistic fortunes inside them. You know the type: "Great success is just around the corner." Obviously, there's nothing to this. However, that evening I was thrown off by the, ahem, "fortune" my son received: "A good way to keep healthy is to eat Chinese food." I had two thoughts about this. First, that's hilarious. Second, that isn't a fortune; it's an instruction, a call to action. It does not proclaim some vague forthcoming blessing, but it gives you something to do. It's advice, not a fortune. Good tasting advice, to be sure. But it is not a fortune.

Now, my kids play this game when they get fortune cookies: is this a fortune or an instruction? I've used this to help them learn the difference between law and gospel. Obviously, cheap paper fortunes inside of sweet styrofoam cookies aren't God's word. But these fortunes do offer two kinds of words: instruction and blessing. Imperative sentences and indicative sentences. What troubles me is that they purport to give fortunes (hence the name, *fortune cookie!*) but instead make demands (*order more kung pao!*).

This distinction, as innocuous as it might be when describing fortunes in cookies, is of crucial importance when it comes to our faith. God speaks two words to his people: law words and gospel words. For the Christian—and especially for a preacher—to take law and call it gospel or turn gospel into a command harms the faith of God's people.

DOCTORS OF THEOLOGY

Luther once said that anyone who could properly distinguish law and gospel should be made a doctor of theology.[1] His concern wasn't merely exegetical. It's not hard to learn the difference between a command and a promise, between an imperative that says, "Do this," and an indicative that says, "It's done." To be sure, recognizing these differences opens the Scriptures to faithful understanding. But this wasn't Luther's primary concern when handing out doctorates for theological acumen. He had pastoral care in mind. He was thinking not just of understanding the nature and content of the text but how to proclaim it to sinners. The art of distinguishing law and gospel is worked out in preaching, teaching, and conversation. It's learning to "speak a timely word" (Prov. 15:23).

Failing to distinguish law and gospel in God's word—that is, to preach the proper word at the proper time—can do significant damage to the faith of the Good Shepherd's beloved sheep. After all, the law and the gospel are God's words that he commands his ambassadors to proclaim to his subjects. These words are the voice of the Shepherd that the sheep trust and follow: "My sheep hear my voice, and I know them, and they follow me" (John 10:27). Confusing law and gospel is dangerous because it leads the sheep away from Christ and into pride, despair, or a false sense of security.

Law and gospel can be confused in several ways. I don't have the space to go into all of these,[2] but I will describe four traps we should recognize in order

---

1   Martin Luther, *What Luther Says: A Practical In-Home Anthology for the Active Christian,* compiled by Ewald M Plass (Concordia Publishing House, St. Louis, 1959), 732.

2   Consider one of the great father's of American Lutheranism, CFW Walther. He gave a series of lectures entitled "The Proper Distinction of Law and Gospel" in which he discussed 25 different ways that the law and the

to avoid confusing these two words from God.

TRAP #1: SEPARATING WHAT GOD HAS DISTINGUISHED

The first trap we must avoid is separating law and gospel to such an extreme that they have nothing to say to each other. We must learn to keep the law and the gospel distinct, but they can't be separated.

Though both are words of God, the law and the gospel are different doctrines. The law is a command that depends on the recipient of the word; the gospel is a promise that depends on the speaker of the word. In the former, God expects you to do something. In the latter, God promises to do everything. The law is to be performed, the gospel to be received by the faith it creates. Luther wrote, "As widely as gift differs from an example, so widely does faith differ from works, for faith possesses nothing of its own, only the deeds and life of Christ. Works have something of your own in them, yet should not belong to you but to your neighbor."[3]

These two words must not be confused with each other, but they also can't be understood apart from each other. Jim Nestingen is our teacher here:

> When Law and Gospel are improperly distinguished, both are undermined. Separated from the Law, the Gospel gets absorbed into an ideology of tolerance in which indiscriminateness is equated with grace. Separated from the Gospel, the Law becomes an insatiable demand hammering away at the conscience until it destroys a person.[4]

---

gospel are properly preached and how they are confused. See CFW Walther, *Law and Gospel: How to Read and Apply the Bible* (Concordia Publishing House: St. Louis, 2010). See also John Pless's book, *Handling the Word of Truth*, 9.

3   Martin Luther, "A Brief Instruction on What to Look for in the Gospels," in *Luther's Works, vol. 35: Word and Sacrament I*. (Fortress Press: Philadelphia, 1960), 120.

4   James Arne Nestingen, "Distinguishing Law and Gospel: A Functional View" in *Concordia Journal* 22 (January 1996): 27.

The law leaves us hopeless without the gospel. The gospel makes no sense without the law. If the law is preached alone without the good news of Christ's saving work for sinners, then Christianity becomes just like every other religion. Salvation becomes a matter of morality and obedience on our part. God is nothing other than an exacting judge who gives no quarter and therfore, for sinners, no hope.

The gospel without the law is incomprehensible. Though I agree with Nestingen's assessment, I might add a word of qualification. Separated from the law, the gospel certainly does get absorbed into a liberal ideology that posits a God who is nothing but love. But, a God that is "nothing but love" isn't the good news the gospel proclaims. It's too vague. The nature of that love must be spelled out. In order to speak of a God of love without the law, you must redefine the gospel. The gospel is never merely the idea that "God loves you anyway." Rather, the gospel is the good news that God has put on flesh in order to fulfill the demands of the law and pay the penalty of the law by taking its curses and condemnations on himself. Jesus taking the law's condemnation away from us by absorbing it himself in his bloody death on the cross is the gospel. The gospel says that you, dear reader, are forgiven for your sins. But the gospel never accuses you of those sins. That's the work of the law. You won't know your need of Christ Jesus if he first doesn't show you your sin with his law. The law and the gospel must be kept distinct, but they shouldn't be understood without each other.

TRAP #2: NULLIFICATION BY ADDITION

The second trap we must avoid is seeking to enhance the work of the gospel by adding the law to it. This trap says the gospel is incomplete for me until I contribute my work. In this trap, the law and the gospel aren't separated but instead smashed together, and Christ is seen as insufficient.

Writing to the Galatians, Paul showed passionate concern about distinguishing law and gospel. He worried about the saints in these congregations being led astray by false teachers who undermined the preaching of Jesus Christ as our righteousness. Paul implied that the false teachers were nullifying the gospel by adding to it. They added to the gospel by preaching the need for circumcision which, of course, would lead the Galatians back to a life under the law and not under grace. He said, "I do not nullify the grace of God, for if righteousness were through the law, then Christ died for no purpose" (Gal. 2:21).

Notice how the nullification of the gospel takes place: by the addition of the law. The Judaizers, Paul's enemies, were quite slick. They moved into the congregations started under Paul's apostolic authority and said, "This was a great start! Isn't the work of Jesus amazing? His dying and rising has started your salvation. Now, to be fully saved and completely righteous, you must organize your life in compliance with the regulations of the old covenant. The promise of baptism isn't enough; you need to be circumcised.[5] Faith is insufficient for righteousness. You need to get to work!"

Paul says that this teaching nullifies the grace of God. It confuses law and gospel by preaching a word in addition to the gospel is required for justification. It teaches you to trust the law—a weight the law can't carry. If you trust in the law, you're really trusting in your works, your performance, your self. You're left wondering if you've done enough, worked enough, been circumcised enough. Here is where adverbs begin to poison pure faith: are you *truly* repentant? Did you give your heart to God *fully*? Have you made Jesus the Lord of your life *completely* or only in part? Such preaching fixes your eyes and your faith not on Jesus, the author and finisher of your faith (Heb. 5:9), but on your ability to keep the law. It's a recipe for despair, the opposite of faith.

---

5 It's worth noting that Paul's treatment of baptism always sets it in terms of the gospel and not the law. Circumcision belongs to the category of works, whereas baptism is in the category of gifts and promises. Paul doesn't see baptism as merely a new identity marker, like circumcision was for the Old Testament people of Israel. Rather, it's a promise from God to give Christ Jesus and all his benefits to the recipient.

This trap nullifies the gospel in the hearts of God's people because it adds something to it. By adding circumcision or any work of ours to the gospel, we subtract from it. What's taken away? Jesus! "If righteousness were through the law, then Christ died for no purpose" (Gal. 2:21). If we contribute to our salvation, Jesus's death for the forgiveness of sins is incomplete and pointless.

When it comes to our salvation, the law has done its job when it tells us we've sinned and fallen short of the glory of God (Rom. 3:23). That's all the law has to say to sinners before God. But Christ moves in and says of the law's condemnations against you, "It is finished" (John 19:30). Christ stands before God as the full and final propitiation for your sins. He stands between you and God with the work of your salvation complete, with no help from your obedience to the law, thank you very much. Standing between you and God, He moves into your conscience to wash it clean and remove your guilt and shame. He reigns in mercy before God and in your conscience. Adding anything to this takes away from all of it.

TRAP #3: CALLING A THING WHAT IT ISN'T

Related to the ways we nullify the gospel by addition is the danger that comes from ascribing the responsibilities of the law to the gospel and vice versa. We fall into this trap when we make salvation, which is the work of Christ in the gospel, dependent on the law (as we saw in the previous section) or when works of love toward our neighbors are called the gospel. Let's examine the danger that arises when we call our works the gospel.

It has been demonstrated that St. Francis of Assisi never said his most famous quote, "Preach the gospel and when necessary use words." This idea is a of distorted version of James 2:17: "So also faith by itself, if it does not have works, is dead." James warned against using the gospel as an excuse to get out of loving their neighbor. A problem to be sure! But equally dangerous is the idea that when one loves his neighbor he has done the work of the gospel even if he hasn't mentioned Jesus Christ. Such love for one's neighbor may be good and temporally beneficial, but it does not give the gift of faith, the promise of forgiveness, and the good news of what Jesus Christ has done for that neighbor. The focus becomes my love and not Christ's salvation. I might be giving daily bread to my neighbor, but if I do not preach the forgiveness of Jesus into his ears, I've starved him of salvation.

Our work isn't the gospel. Only Jesus saves. How arrogant of us to think that our works can be so loving, so righteous, so glorious that others will come to faith in Jesus because of our performance. If you really think your works are good enough to bring others to Christ, ask your spouse or your closest friends how impressive you are! Your good works can't save you, so how do you expect them to save others?

Good deeds are important. They are fruits of the Spirit that flow from the life of the one who has been saved by God's grace alone. But they aren't gospel for you or anyone else. God alone does gospel work. To be sure, Jesus says people will see our good deeds and so praise our Father in heaven (Matt 5:16). But how will they know of that Father unless someone preaches to them? What's more, how will they know about the divine Son of that Father and his saving work unless we open our mouths and proclaim repentance and the forgiveness of sins? As Paul says, "Faith comes through hearing, and hearing through the word of Christ" (Rom. 10:17).

Here, such a view of the law's role in our lives silences the gospel and produces pride in our own works. Pride is the other opposite of faith. The good news is that you do not do the gospel, you preach the gospel. Your good works are good for your neighbor; they aren't the gospel of salvation for your neighbor. It is only the incarnation, dying, rising, and reigning of Jesus Christ that saves. But no one will know it until you take this message and hand it over. So, preach the gospel, and, when necessary, use your deeds to love your neighbor.

The final trap we must avoid is making God nice. This trap is "antinomianism," a five-dollar theological word that means one sees no need for the law in the life of the Christian. It's a theology that says, "It doesn't matter who you are or what you've done, God loves you anyway." As we saw earlier, the broad claim that God loves you isn't the gospel. It's true that God loves you, and no one's sins are too big for the grace of God in Christ, but this claim is easily misunderstood—and dangerously so.

To portray God as a nice God who doesn't care about who you are or what you've done makes God's commands meaningless. His word loses all its bite. Would God truly be loving if he didn't care that a person has harmed others? If God doesn't care about our sin, why is Jesus so furious with the religious leaders placing burdens on people's backs that they were unable to carry? Would God truly be loving if he didn't care about unjust war, racism, the destruction of the family, abusive clergy, and other sins? If God truly loves his creation and his creatures, he can't love without being just.

Further, such a stance is impossible to hold. No one can truly maintain an antinomian position. Soon, those who cling tightest to the "God loves me anyway" creed will be the ones defending immorality as a right and condemning Biblical preachers for their archaic and oppressive dogmatism. Gerhard Forde was right when he said that antinomianism is a fake theology.[6]

This is the sort of theology Paul warns us will come in the last days. He says, "For the time is coming when people will not endure sound teaching, but having itching ears they will accumulate for themselves teachers to suit their own passions, and will turn away from the truth to wander off into myths" (2 Tim. 4:3–4). People desire a God who will cater to their desires, who will tell

---

6   Gerhard Forde, "Fake Theology: Reflections on Antinomianism Past and Present" in *Dialog* 22, no. 4 (Fall 1983): 246–251.

them encouraging words to assist them on their way to self-realization. They want a nice life-coach of a god.

This is a god, however, who has no real law and therefore no gospel. Teachers who offer such gods are Jeremiah's false prophets, crying "peace, peace" all the way to God's judgment. Such teachers lead people to God, teaching them to trust that God will give their performance the benefit of the doubt, only to hand them over to God with no faith and no Christ, and therefore, no hope.

One can't get out from under the judgment of the law by pretending God doesn't judge. The law is an objective reality, not a culturally conditioned idea that we can adjust to suit our whims. Our only hope before this judgment isn't that a nice God will grade on a curve but that a righteous God has saved us from condemnation by dealing with our sins himself. So, Christ Jesus came, born under the law to redeem those under the law (Gal. 4:4). He suffered and died for our sins in order to be both just and the justifier of the ungodly (Rom. 3:25–26).

Martin Chemnitz writes:

> Therefore the righteousness of the Law and of the Gospel is different, and it is also the same. In respect to us it is different, cf. Phil. 3:9, "a righteousness which is not of the Law." But with respect to Christ it is the same; for what the Law demands and requires, this Christ supplies and gives. So also reconciliation is called redemption with respect to Christ because the compensation has been paid; but with respect to us it is called the gracious remission of sins."[7]

You'll often hear this watered-down version of the gospel. It presents God as "love" apart from the loving action of the Father sending the Son who

---

7 Martin Chemnitz, *Justification: The Chief Article of Christian Doctrine as Expounded in Loci Theologici.* Tr. JAO Preus (Concordia: St. Louis, 1985), 36.

willingly came to die for the sins of the world and suffer the wrath we deserved. Preaching atonement-free love creates space for sin to go undealt with. It removes repentance and muffles the voice of the Good Shepherd who calls out to stop his sheep from wandering into a den of wolves. It leads sinners before God's tribunal without a savior.

CONCLUSION

These four traps are only a few of the ways we can confuse the law and the gospel. In order to avoid these and any other traps that may come our way, it's best that we just let God's word speak for itself. The preacher's job is to preach the text—the law and the gospel—and then get out of the way. God the Holy Spirit, after all, knows what he's doing with his word. He has graciously given us his word as a lamp to our feet and light to our path (Ps. 119:105). Both the law and the gospel are those glorious lights that lead us to Christ. The law shows us our sin and our need for a savior. The good news for you is that God in Christ has paid for your sins with his own blood. He's your Savior. The great challenge for every preacher—and for every Christian—is to fight the temptation to confuse God's commands and judgments with the blood-bought and graciously given promises of Christ Jesus.

And, now, back to the Chinese food!

CHAPTER FIVE

The Righteousness of Faith and the Righteousness of the Law

Robert M. Hiller

I REMEMBER WATCHING A TELEVISION SHOW WHERE a person who had carried out some morally suspect activities got caught in their sins. When confronted by others about what he had done, the accused cried out, "I don't care what you say! Only God can judge me!" Now, I'm not in a position to speak to the theological background of this person. But two things struck me about this "defense." First, as a dyed-in-the-wool, law/gospel-loving Lutheran, I shuddered at the presumption that God's judgment was good news. Perhaps this person was appealing to the shed blood of Christ for their forgiveness, but that wasn't what he said. Instead, he implied that God would be on his side, that God would judge his actions as righteous. Pleading one's case before God with no appeal to Christ is not a safe place to stand.

However, the second thing that struck me was this: by appealing to God's judgment, this person brought up something that's lost on our society. For as foolhardy as it is for someone to appeal to God to approve of their sin, at least this person recognized that, ultimately, it is God alone who is to judge. And his judgment is true; it is just; it is righteous.

This answer strikes me because God, let alone his judgment, does not seem to matter much anymore. As Robert Kolb has pointed out, ours is not a day where we fear God's judgment; rather, we demand that God justify himself to us.[1] The fear of God's righteous wrath that terrified the sixteenth century does not weigh heavily on the twenty-first-century conscience.

Yet it is not hard to see that everyone seeks their own justification—if not before God then before the world. Social media is an exercise in judging the specks in others' eyes while boasting about the logs in our own. News stations no longer just report the news but instead tell us how to judge each story. Consider ESPN, a television station that came to prominence with SportsCenter, a sports news show that features game highlights. Now, ESPN's talking heads debate "hot takes" on everything taking place on and off the field. These televised op-ed arguments judge events which we, in turn, either agree with or condemn. One can't even look for sports highlights without entering in the game of justification.[2]

Everyone fights for righteousness and acceptance before some tribunal. And, though our God-forsaking culture seeks justification in both important and trivial way before the world, all must stand before God on the day of judgment. On that day each of us will give an account of ourselves to God (Rom. 14:12). Our televised friend is right that God will judge us, but on what basis can we have any hope before his tribunal? Who can ascend the hill of the Lord with any sense of confidence? (Ps. 24:3) Further, one may wonder: is it true that only God's judgment matters? Is there not a righteousness in this world that we ought to aspire to?

---

1   Robert Kolb, "Luther on the Theology of the Cross" in *The Pastoral Luther: Essays on Martin Luther's Practical Theology,* ed. Timothy Wengert (Eerdmans Publishing: Grand Rapids, 2009), 33–56. The issues of theodicy are well beyond the scope of this little article. I heartily recommend Kolb's essay as a helpful guide in using Luther's theology of the cross as a framework for addressing these contemporary theological problems.

2   For more on the ways in which so much of our world is shaped by the language of justification see Oswald Bayer, *Living by Faith: Justification and Sanctification* (Eerdmans Publishing: Grand Rapids, 2003). For a less academic, but more enjoyable read on this topic, see David Zahl, *Seculosity: How Career, Parenting, Technology, Food, Politics, and Romance Became Our New Religion and What to Do about It* (Broadleaf: Minneapolis, 2019).

In answer to these questions, the Reformers presented a helpful framework for understanding how one is declared righteous (justified). In the introduction to Luther's great Galatians commentary, the Reformer draws a distinction between two kinds of righteousness: active righteousness, or the righteousness of the law, and the passive righteousness of Christ— the righteousness of faith. "This is our theology, by which we teach a precise distinction between these two kinds of righteousness, the active and the passive, so that morality and faith, works and grace, secular society and religion may not be confused."[3]

We could say that passive righteousness has to do with our standing before God (*coram Deo*) and active righteousness has to do with our activity in the world (*coram mundo*). One is found righteous before God in an entirely different way than one is found righteous before their neighbor. In the former instance, justification is declared freely on account of Christ; in the latter, it is earned by the work that you do for the sake of your neighbor.

The distinction between these two kinds of righteousness is not to be confused with the distinction between law and gospel, which we have been examining in this booklet. But the distinctions are certainly related. Law and gospel are the words of God that he speaks to us in terms of commands and promises. The two kinds of righteousness describe the way we relate to God and the world. In these given relationships, the law and the gospel have specific functions for our righteousness. How one is rendered righteous before God is a matter of the gospel and how one is justified in the world is a matter of the law. But in both realms God has something to say with his law and gospel, so we have something to hear. Law and gospel have something to say to you in your relationship to God and your neighbor.

---

3   Martin Luther, "Lectures on Galatians 1535, Chapters 1–4," in *Luther's Works (LW)* 26 (Concordia Publishing House: St. Louis, 1963), 7.

In your relationship to God, the law demands perfect righteousness, but it does not give it. In this conversation, the law takes the form of command and accusation. It functions here in two ways. First, it shows you what you must do to meet the conditions of righteousness: "If you do this, you will live." Consider Psalm 15 from the perspective of the Law:

> O Lord, who shall sojourn in your tent? Who shall dwell on your holy hill? He who walks blamelessly and does what is right and speaks truth in his heart; who does not slander with his tongue and does no evil to his neighbor, nor takes up a reproach against his friend; in whose eyes a vile person is despised, but who honors those who fear the Lord; who swears to his own hurt and does not change; who does not put out his money at interest and does not take a bribe against the innocent. He who does these things shall never be moved. (Ps. 15)

Here is what is expected of you in the law: blamelessness in thought, word, and deed. Clean hands, clean mouth, clean mind, clean heart. This describes the righteous person whom God's law declares innocent. And it is not you.

The second thing—and really the main thing—the law does to us before God is expose us as sinners. The demands of the law, as laid out in Psalm 15, offer no hope. "The Law came in," writes Paul, "so that the trespass would increase" (Rom. 5:20). Thus, before God the law's primary work is to show you your unrighteousness. Before God, our good works and obedience to the law avail us nothing. Even the best of our good works are rendered unclean. God's judgment is confessed in Isaiah, "all our righteous deeds are like a polluted garment" (Isa. 64:6).

Good works in the eyes of the world become the worst of sins before God when we bring them into his presence expecting a reward. When someone seeks to be justified by obedience to the law, when someone ascends the mountain of the Lord to prove how clean their hands are, they are forgetting their position before God. One would be saying to God, "I've met your standards; I have met your demands; now you owe me!" In this situation, we're actually seeking to put God in our debt! The law is not given as something to trust. Good works are not performed in order to earn God's favor. Before God, the law is never satisfied by our good works and to presume otherwise is the height of sin.

To summarize the word of the law before God, Luther writes,

> The foremost office or power of the law is that it reveals inherited sin and its fruits. It show human beings into what utter depths their nature has fallen and how completely corrupt it is. The law must say to them that they neither have nor respect any god or that they worship foreign gods. This is something that they would not have believed without the law. They are terrified, humbled, despondent, and despairing.[4]

Here, then, the law leaves us for dead. But such work is necessary, for only when we are dead will we be ready for Christ to raise us to a new life. Luther again, "Now this is the thunderbolt of God, by means of which he destroys both the open sinner and false saint. And allows no one to be right but drives the whole of them into terror and despair . . . . This is really what it means to begin true repentance."[5] God does not speak his law to us with the aim of leaving us accused and condemned. Accusing with the law is strange speech for God, whose primary work is to be gracious and kind to his beloved creatures. But it is necessary to awaken the sinner to the depths of their sin and rebellion so that they will cease from trusting in their own righteousness and despair of their works. Once God gets them to this point, he is ready to speak an entirely different word altogether: a word of gospel.

---

4   Martin Luther, "The Smalcald Articles (SA) III:2," *The Book of Concord* (Fortress Press: Minneapolis, 2000), 312.

5   SA III:3.

Before God, the Law has left us for dead. But now, God shows up to raise the dead. "Those who are well have no need of a physician, but those who are sick. I came not to call the righteous, but sinners" (Mark 2:17). Notice how the direction changes. In Psalm 15, we see the law describing the upward movement of the would-be saint, but in the gospel we hear of God coming down to sinners dead in their guilt. He comes to impart a righteousness "apart from the Law" (Rom. 3:21). With this word, God makes no demands and renders no accusations against you. This is a word that silences the law before God. It's the gospel, the good news, that God has graciously chosen to forgive sinners solely by the dying and rising of Jesus Christ and to give that forgiveness to them in preaching and sacrament.

After the law has left us thoroughly convinced that there is no active righteousness for us before God, the gospel proclaims a passive righteousness rendered by grace alone to faith alone. Faith receives this righteousness; our works do not earn it:

> But God, being rich in mercy, because of the great love with which he loved us, even when we were dead in our trespasses, made us alive together with Christ—by grace you have been saved—and raised us up with him and seated us with him in the heavenly places in Christ Jesus, so that in the coming ages he might show the immeasurable riches of his grace in kindness toward us in Christ Jesus. (Eph. 2:4–7)

The dead have a hard time climbing out of the grave to work toward righteousness. It is God—who is rich in mercy—who makes us alive. He declares sinners righteous by his grace alone: "And to the one who does not work but believes in him who justifies the ungodly, his faith is counted as righteousness" (Rom. 4:5).

So, does God just dismiss the law with the gospel and pretend like our sins never took place? What becomes of our guilt and our sin? Is justice ignored for the sake of mercy? As attractive as that last question may be, we must understand that God does not deal in abstractions. Rather, our sin is an offense against God's righteousness that deserves his punishment. And his mercy is not some ideal that God seeks to achieve in his attitude toward us. Rather, it is his action carried out in the life, death, and resurrection of the incarnate Son. God is merciful in sending Jesus Christ to die as an atoning sacrifice for your sins and thus declares you righteous on his account. Sin is dealt with in Christ. Faith clings to this for its righteousness.

Philip Melanchthon, in his Apology (Defense) of the Augsburg Confession, says that the righteousness of faith requires three things:

> The promise itself, the fact that the promise is free; and the merits of Christ as the payment and atoning sacrifice. The promise is received by faith; the word 'free' excludes our merits and means that the blessing is offered only through mercy; the merits of Christ are the payment because there must be some definite atoning sacrifice for our sins.[6]

This is an important point. One is not righteous before God without God promising to give that righteousness as a free gift. And that gift is not available unless it is purchased with the blood of Christ. Our righteousness before God is not based on our performance but on Jesus's work for us. It is outside of us but given to us. Because you and I are sinners, the law will never call us righteous. But Jesus put on our flesh and became our brother (John 1:14, Heb. 7:25–28). He was like us completely, yet without sin, so he was able to offer up his life as a sacrifice to pay for our sins. He was the perfect Lamb of God who takes away the sin of the world (John 1:29). Actively, he perfectly obeyed God's will and thus fulfilled the law. Jesus is the man of Psalm 15! Passively, he suffered and

---

6 "The Apology of the Augsburg Confession (Ap.) IV: 53," in *The Book of Concord* (Fortress Press: Minneapolis, 2000), 128–129.

died in the place of sinners and thus absorbed all of the law's condemnation. In this way, Jesus is the end of the law (Rom. 10:4). He kept it and suffered under its judgments for your sins so that the law can no longer condemn you. There is no condemnation left for you (Rom. 8:1).

This is no mere historical event, though it took place under Pontius Pilate. This saving of Christ was done for you. It is news that Jesus did this. It is good news (gospel) that he has done it for us—for you. Faith is not mere historical knowledge of what Jesus has done. Faith is what happens when you receive the news and are told, "Jesus did that for you. Your sins were the very sins he took credit for. You are the very person he credits with his righteousness." Faith is created by this promise and faith trusts this promise. In this way, faith, not works of the law, is credited with righteousness: "It will be counted to us who believe in him who raised from the dead Jesus our Lord, who was delivered up for our trespasses and raised for our justification" (Rom. 4:24–25).

Our righteousness before God is in Christ alone. Christ died to take away the sins that render us unrighteous and was raised from the dead to declare us forgiven, righteous, justified. The law is not there to earn us that verdict; it no longer has anything to say about us before God. You and I have this promise—given for free—that Christ has fulfilled the law in our place; has paid our sins' debt in our place; has forgiven, reconciled, and redeemed us to make us righteous before God: "Christ is the end of the law for righteousness to everyone who believes" (Rom. 10:4). To use a well-worn phrase, you are righteous by grace alone, through faith alone, on account of Christ alone.

LAW CORAM MUNDO

So, what then? What becomes of the law and good works? Have they no place but to accuse us? Though it is true that the law always accuses, it also gives order to society, keeps sinners in check with its threats, and grants temporal rewards with its promises—conditional promises to be sure, but promises nonetheless. The law cannot make sinners righteous before God, but it is good at showing us how to conduct our lives in this world—how to serve our neighbors in our vocations.

Good works cannot to replace Christ. We cannot trust them for our salvation. If we do, they become idols. Instead, we do good out of love for our neighbors. Conversely, the righteousness of faith avails before God, but it does me no good in righteousness before my neighbor. Your salvation does not put food on the table for your kids to eat. Your salvation does not get you out of paying your taxes. You cannot skip three days of work with no notice, let down your colleagues, waste your company's money and then say to your boss, "Don't worry! I'm saved by the blood of Christ!" Your boss will rightly reply, "Great! Also, you're fired." The righteousness of faith is not an excuse to keep you from loving your neighbor.

Faith belongs in our relationship with God and receives gifts. Love belongs to our neighbor and does work. Here, that dictum often attributed to Luther is helpful, "God does not need your good works, but your neighbor does."[7] The law guides us as we carry out our responsibilities as creatures towards other creatures in God's good creation. In this realm, righteousness is by works and can be performed by Christians and non-Christians alike. The Reformers can go so far as to say even the pagan philosophers, who know nothing of the righteousness of faith, can speak of righteousness achieved in this world, "After all, Aristotle wrote so eruditely about social ethics that nothing needs to be added." [8]

In the world, righteousness is not concerned as much with the attitude of your heart or the location of your faith as it is with the works of your hands. C. S. Lewis offers wonderful advice here: "Do not waste time bothering whether you 'love' your neighbor; act as if you did. As soon as we do this we find one

---

7 Gustaf Wingren, *Luther on Vocation,* tr. Carl C. Rasmussen (Wipf & Stock: Eugene. 2004), 10.

8 Ap. IV.14, 122.

of the great secrets. When you are behaving as if you loved someone, you will presently come to love him."[9] The point here is to do what God has given you to do whether your heart is in it or not. You show your child you love them not by feeding them only when your heart is driven purely by love but instead when it is dinner time. In the world, your motives matter little; your neighbor's need and God's command to serve are what matter.

What works, then, should be done in this world? Who is the neighbor I am to love? Because Christians wrestle with that old, sinful flesh, we have a tendency to want to pursue a greater righteousness than those in the world around us. So, the old sinner will invent holier, more righteous works than God prescribes for the rest of the world. We'll enter the monastary or burn our secular albums and only buy "Christian" music or advertise that we are "Christian" plumbers. But here is where the law keeps us in check by telling us God's will. It tells us which works God expects. The Lutheran Reformers wrote, "For this reason, too, believers require the teaching of the law; so that they do not fall back on their own holiness and piety and under the appearance of God's Spirit establish their own service to God on the basis of their own choice, without God's Word or command."[10]

God has given us three estates in this world for us to carry out our works according to his law: the church, the household, and the government. In these places, God has given us neighbors and commands. In the church, God gives his gifts of word and sacrament. Our job is to worship, to look after the pastor's needs so he can faithfully preach, and to look after the needs of our brothers and sisters with the gifts God has given us. The pastor's job is to faithfully preach and teach, visit the shut-ins and sick, administer the sacraments, call for repentance, and deliver forgiveness.

---

9   C.S. Lewis, *Mere Christianity* (Touchstone: New York. 1996), 11.

10 "The Solid Declaration of the Formula of Concord (SD)," in *The Book of Concord,* Article VI:20 (Fortress Press: Minneapolis, 2000), 590.

The household consists of the family and the workplace. Here we concern ourselves with the second table of the law. We work hard for our family members, honoring parents and training up children in the way they should go. At work, we serve our bosses as the Lord, pay our employees a fair wage, make our jobs less burdensome for our coworkers by doing our job well, and serve our customers by producing quality products.

The government exists to keep order in society. Here God works through the magistrates to punish the evildoer and reward moral, upstanding citizens (Rom. 13). As citizens, we work to honor those in authority. We also find ways to care for the poor, fight for justice, and work for a just and honorable society. This work will look different depending on the context and circumstances of the society. There is no established form of government given by God in the New Testament that Christians are to establish; rather, whatever country Christians find themselves in, they are to work for peace, love, and justice.

Now, in all of these areas, God's law serves to both curb sin with its threats and promises and to guide the Christian in righteous living. It will never give perfection because it is still carried out by sinners. No church, no family, and certainly no state will ever be perfect this side of the resurrection. Our job is not to pursue perfection in these areas, but to love our neighbors according to God's law. Further, even in the world, the law is never satisfied. Sin still corrupts even our best efforts and Satan is happy to wreak havoc in our lives. Even here, the law shows us our sins and weaknesses and drives us to Christ for assurance and strength.

GOSPEL CORAM MUNDO

Given that righteousness before the world is not based on faith but performance, one may be tempted to think that the gospel has little to say here. After all, by the judgment of the world, a non-Christian may at times look just as righteous as the Christian—if not more so—because their works may be more effective. God works through the righteous and the unrighteous to keep order in the world.

And yet the gospel that renders one righteous before God continues to grant gifts and blessings to the Christian who is at work in God's creation. The gospel impacts the Christian as they work in the world in at least three ways. First, the good news of Jesus makes us altogether new creatures who cannot help but do good works.[11] Faith, after all, works through love (Gal. 5:6). Christ has given his Holy Spirit to the believer who then becomes an instrument of love. The Christian's good works are truly the fruit of the Spirit himself (Gal. 5:22–24). One who is righteous before God has become a branch on the vine, who is Christ. Apart from him, we can do nothing, but when united to him, he produces all sorts of good works in our lives (John 15:1–17). The Formula of Concord quotes Luther: "Thus it is impossible to separate works from faith, quite as impossible as it is to separate heat and light from fire."[12]

Second, the gospel frees me to love my neighbor without fear of God's wrath. If righteousness before God is by my obedience to the law and my performance, then my neighbor ceases to be an object of my love and becomes a means to an end: namely, my righteousness. I will no longer love my neighbor but use him. I will only work for my neighbor in ways that benefit me. What benefits me is what is impressive and glorious. Works of love become nothing more than photo opportunities for my heavenly resume. My good works become an opportunity for pride.

The flip side is that work for my neighbor, in that case, is not carried out in the freedom of God's grace. Instead, I work out of fear. If I do not love my neighbor the right way, if I sin against them or act too selfishly or fail in my responsibility in any way, all hope is lost. If my work in the world is the basis of my righteousness before God, I am left in despair for my salvation.

---

11 SD IV:10–12.

12 SD IV:12.

The gospel frees us from such pride and fear. Your neighbor does not exist as an opportunity to earn a reward because God has given you all you need in Christ Jesus. Further, you need not fear how perfectly you perform your works of love in this world, for Christ alone is your righteousness and he has already promised you forgiveness. You are already completely righteous in the eyes of God for his sake, because of his work, not yours. So, you are finally free to love your neighbor without fear, from a heart purified by Christ.

Third, unlike the work of non-Christians who may look good in the eyes of the world, the work you do as a baptized child of God is called good by God. Works carried out apart from faith are sins in God's eyes: "Without faith it is impossible to please [God]" (Heb. 11:6). But because you have been purchased with the blood of Christ and you are righteous through faith, God sees your works and calls them good. Charles Arand says, "Faith must be regarded as the presupposition for good works."[13] The acts of love you perform, though neither trustworthy for righteousness nor done for the sake of reward, are yet pleasing to God by his gracious decision alone. Though you may not see the good works you are doing clearly, God sees them as righteous because he has declared you righteous for Christ's sake. Your works are good according to God so that you can hear already now, before Christ returns, the promised blessing of God which he will speak over his people on the last day, "Well done, good and faithful servant. You have been faithful over a little; I will set you over much. Enter into the joy of your master" (Matt. 25:21, 23)

CONCLUSION

Summarizing these two kinds of righteousness, Luther says, "We conclude, therefore, that a Christian lives not in himself, but in Christ and in his neighbor. Otherwise he is not a Christian. He lives in Christ through faith, in his neighbor

---

13 Charles Arand, "Two Kinds of Righteousness as a Framework for Law and Gospel in the Apology." *Lutheran Quarterly* XV (Winter 2001), 417–439.

through love. By faith he is caught up beyond himself into God. By love he descends beneath himself into his neighbor."[14] Christians then live in a vertical relationship with God and horizontal relationships with their neighbors. God has something to say with both his law and his gospel to his baptized pilgrims as they carry out their lives before him and with their neighbors. And it is these words of law and gospel that will inform and sustain us until Christ comes again and we, by grace alone, will enter into his eternal joy:

> Then they will need neither the proclamation of the law nor its threats and punishment, just as they will no longer need the gospel, for both belong to this imperfect life. Instead, just as they will see God face-to-face, so they will perform the will of God by the power of the indwelling Spirit of God spontaneously, without coercion, unhindered, perfectly and completely, with sheer joy, and they will delight in his will eternally.[15]

---

14 Martin Luther, *The Freedom of the Christian* in *LW* 31 (Fortress Press: Philadelphia, 1957), 371.

15 SD VI:24-25, 591.

More Church Resources *Available*

LEAD A GROUP WITH
SOLA BIBLE STUDIES

Our growing library of Bible studies will take you deep into God's word in ten lessons. They're perfect for individual use, small groups, Sunday school, and community outreach. Leader's editions are available for all our studies, making it easier for you to lead a group.

New Testament	*Old Testament*	*Topical Studies*
Galatians	Daniel	Core Christianity 101
Hebrews	Jonah	
John	Ruth	How to Read the Bible
Luke		
Philippians		The Nicene Creed
Romans		
Revelation		Parables

Get the latest Sola videos, podcasts, articles, and more in your inbox. www.solamedia.org/subscribe

MORE RESOURCES TO
AID DISCIPLESHIP

Designed to help people find answers to common questions and dig deeper into foundational truths, our booklets are ideal tools for discipleship. Typically less than 100 pages and always written by trusted authors, these booklets provide rich, accessible content for personal reflection and group discussion.

Booklets

What Is God's
Will for Me?

What is
Secularization?

Can the Devil
Read My Mind?

Law & Gospel

How to Keep Your
Faith After High
School

Why Would Anyone
Get Married?

Seeing Jesus

Made in the USA
Columbia, SC
31 October 2024

45345274R00033